IMAGES
of America

TULSA

OIL CAPITAL OF THE WORLD

Standing tall in front of the Tulsa Exposition Center on East 21st Street, the Golden Driller was built for display during the International Petroleum Exposition (IPE). A plaque states that the statue, presented by Mid-Continent Supply Co. on May 12, 1966, was "dedicated to the men of the petroleum industry who by their vision and daring have created from God's abundance a better life for mankind." After being refurbished it was later rededicated as the symbol of Tulsa, "Oil Capital of the World," and of the oil industry and the IPE. By an act of the Legislature, the Golden Driller became Oklahoma's official state monument.

IMAGES
of America

TULSA

OIL CAPITAL OF THE WORLD

James O. Kemm

ARCADIA
PUBLISHING

Published by Arcadia Publishing
Charleston, South Carolina

Library of Congress Catalog Card Number: 2004110524

For all general information contact Arcadia Publishing at:
Telephone 843-853-2070
Fax 843-853-0044
E-mail sales@arcadiapublishing.com
For customer service and orders:
Toll-Free 1-888-313-2665

Visit us on the Internet at www.arcadiapublishing.com

Tulsa's title of "Oil Capital of the World" remained unchallenged for decades as the city became the metropolitan hub of what was called the "Magic Empire." Postcards such as this one helped sustain Tulsa's Oil Capital reputation. Even more important was the attention drawn to Tulsa by its International Petroleum Exposition, which attracted visitors from many oil-producing nations.

CONTENTS

ACKNOWLEDGMENTS

After the American Petroleum Institute transferred me to Tulsa from Kansas City more than a half-century ago, I started collecting old postcards of oil fields, gushers, tank fires, and other Oklahoma petroleum scenes. I continued to accumulate such cards after becoming executive manager of the Oklahoma Petroleum Council five years later. Many images from that collection are used in this book, along with photographs I have taken of oil installations and people in the Tulsa area. Other photographs have been provided by museums, libraries, oil associations, companies, and individuals.

This book is not intended to be a history of the Tulsa oil industry; it is instead an assortment of images of some of the places, people, and happenings related to petroleum in the Tulsa area during the past century. Some photographs and postcards of Muskogee, Bartlesville, Okmulgee, Cushing, Drumright, and other towns within a 50-mile radius of Tulsa have also been included. Tulsa companies and individuals were heavily involved in oil exploration and production in each of those places.

I thank especially the following for providing photographs and assistance: William Welge, director of research, Oklahoma Historical Society; Mary Moore, Tulsa City-County Library; Kathy Seibold, Tulsa Historical Society; and Pam Webb of the Mid-Continent Oil & Gas Association of Oklahoma. Credit is provided in captions for photographs they supplied and for those provided by other organizations, companies, and individuals. To each of those who have been so generous with their assistance, I give my heartfelt thanks.

I also express my appreciation to Melissa Basilone, my editor at Arcadia Publishing, for her advice and help throughout the process of publishing this book. Most of all, I appreciate my wife of 57 years, Betty Ann, for her continuing support and assistance, and our daughters, Kathy Doss, Martha Barrett, and Nancy Pomerantz, for their encouragement and cooperation.

Postcards and photographs not otherwise credited are from my personal collection.

–James O. Kemm
Tulsa, Oklahoma

INTRODUCTION

To many people, the words "Oklahoma" and "oil" are synonymous. This is especially true in reference to Tulsa, the state's second largest city, which for more than seven decades, beginning in the early 1900s, was "The Oil Capital of the World." The title at first seemed boastful for what was then a small Indian Territory town. Before long, however, with the rising popularity of gasoline-powered automobiles, the petroleum industry became more important to the state and the nation, and Tulsa's claim to fame was justified.

The first commercial oil well in what was to become Oklahoma was the Nellie Johnstone No. 1 at Bartlesville, which blew in on April 15, 1897. After that, drilling took place in other parts of Indian Territory.

The first producing oil well in what is now Tulsa County was the Sue A. Bland, drilled by two physicians, Dr. Fred S. Clinton and Dr. J.C. Bland, at Red Fork, just west of Tulsa across the Arkansas River. Completed on June 25, 1901, it erupted as a gusher 36 feet high. Although it produced only four barrels of oil a day, it attracted nationwide attention, and other wells were soon drilled nearby. After three Tulsa oilmen financed the construction of a much-needed bridge across the Arkansas River in 1904 to link Tulsa with Red Fork, Tulsa was on its way to becoming an important oil center.

The validity of Tulsa's claim to the Oil Capital of the World title became apparent after Robert Galbreath, with the financial help of Frank Chesley, drilled the discovery well for the Glenn Pool, the first major oil field in what would become the state of Oklahoma. Called the Ida Glenn No. 1, the well about 12 miles southwest of Tulsa blew in as a gusher on November 22, 1905. It proved to be a historic date, focusing worldwide attention on Tulsa, Indian Territory.

By the time the territory was united with Oklahoma Territory to become the nation's 46th state on November 16, 1907, nearly 100 oil companies were active in the Glenn Pool area. As time went by, Tulsa became the headquarters for companies that were household words, headed by such oil giants as J. Paul Getty, William G. Skelly, Josh Cosden, and William K. Warren. Some of the most famous oil pioneers got their start at Glenn Pool, making fortunes there and sometimes losing them. Nationwide publicity focused attention on Tulsa, and hundreds of independent operators and company executives moved to the growing city. As Glenn Pool drilling expanded and important discoveries occurred in surrounding counties in such places as Osage County and the Cushing-Drumright field, Tulsa oilmen became heavily involved in their development. It was Tulsa that benefited most from the northeastern Oklahoma oil activity.

Tulsa's worldwide reputation was enhanced by several factors. The *Oil & Gas Journal*, the industry's leading trade magazine with worldwide circulation, was published in Tulsa. National and international petroleum associations and scientific societies established their headquarters in the city. Especially important was the 1923 creation of the International Petroleum Exposition in Tulsa. From humble beginnings, the IPE grew into the world's largest trade show, bringing oilmen from many nations to Tulsa throughout its 56-year history.

Petroleum was Tulsa's largest industry, and local citizens took great pride in their city as it developed into a metropolis. National publications called Tulsa "America's cleanest city" and "America's most beautiful city."

Many Tulsans who made fortunes in the oil fields donated large sums of money for the betterment of the city, establishing museums, parks, hospitals, funds for education and charities, and countless other worthwhile enterprises. This trend continues as Tulsa and the nearby town of Glenpool prepare to celebrate the centennial of the Glenn Pool discovery. In the latter part of the 20th century and early 2000s, such oil leaders as John Williams, Henry and Jack Zarrow, and Walt Helmerich III have continued the Tulsa tradition of philanthropy.

Tulsa's role as the Oil Capital of the World became less valid during the 1960s and 1970s when company mergers took place, and the industry began to emphasize offshore drilling. One by one, some of the most recognizable names of companies disappeared from Tulsa, where in many instances they got their start. By 1979, when the Board of Directors of the International Petroleum Exposition decided to close up shop, it had become apparent that with so many companies moving to Houston and other large cities, Tulsa could no longer rightfully call itself the world's oil capital.

But petroleum remains an important part of Tulsa's heritage and its economy. Historical markers and monuments in the city and in other parts of northeast Oklahoma call attention to significant events that have occurred in connection with Tulsa's role in the industry. Many oil companies and other related firms, such as drilling companies and service and supply companies, remain in the city, and new ones have taken the place of some that have moved. Tulsa citizens still benefit from the philanthropy of oil leaders, and the city remains an attractive place to live or visit.

Petroleum has been the driving force in the development of Tulsa and is still a significant part of its economy.

One

EARLY OIL DISCOVERIES

A large stone stands in front of Oklahoma's first commercial oil well in Johnstone Park in Bartlesville, about 50 miles north of Tulsa. The Nellie Johnstone No. 1 well was completed on April 15, 1897, at a depth of 1,320 feet. Its discovery created an excitement that brought about the search for oil in earnest in surrounding areas.

This replica of the Nellie Johnstone No. 1 well was built by the Bartlesville Chamber of Commerce at the original site in 1963. More than 100,000 barrels of oil came from the well before pumping became uneconomical in 1940. In 1997, the energy industry in Oklahoma celebrated its centennial in Bartlesville. (Courtesy Phillips Petroleum Company.)

An early gusher in the Bartlesville field is depicted in this postcard, which shows a wooden derrick similar to the one used in the drilling of Oklahoma's first commercial oil well. The well in this picture produced 100 barrels daily. Rig builders kept busy throughout the oil fields of Indian Territory as the search for oil continued.

The first successful oil well in what would become Tulsa County came in as a producer on June 25, 1901. The well was drilled by two medical doctors, Dr. Fred S. Clinton and Dr. J.C. Bland on the Sue A. Bland homestead adjoining Red Fork, across the Arkansas River from Tulsa in what was then the Creek Nation in Indian Territory. The well, named the Sue A. Bland, erupted as a gusher 36 feet high. Shown at the well site is Dr. Clinton. Within a few hours after the discovery, roads leading to Red Fork, a town that had only about a dozen houses and a few businesses, were crowded with horse-drawn buggies and wagons. Oilmen, bankers, lawyers, speculators, and numerous others rushed to the area by horse, train, and by foot in an effort to strike it rich. (Courtesy Tulsa Historical Society.)

Before there was a wagon bridge linking Tulsa with Red Fork, a ferry enabled passengers to cross the Arkansas River between the two small towns. The width and depth of the Arkansas, which runs through Tulsa just a few blocks from the downtown area, varies according to weather conditions. In later years the Keystone Dam was erected west of Tulsa, permitting the water flow to be regulated. (Courtesy Tulsa Historical Society.)

Often referred to as "The Bridge That Saved Tulsa," this toll bridge across the Arkansas River linking Tulsa with the Red Fork field was completed in 1904. Recognizing the need, three Tulsans (Mel Baird, George T. Williamson, and Don Hagler) put up their own money for the construction, and the bridge opened on January 4, 1904. They put up a sign that read: "They said we couldn't do it but we did." (Courtesy Tulsa Historical Society.)

The first bridge across the Arkansas River in Tulsa was a railroad bridge (in background) built by the St. Louis and San Francisco Railway (known as the "Frisco"). It was completed in 1884 and linked Tulsa with Red Fork. A year later, the railroad line was extended to Sapulpa. In 1904, the toll bridge (in foreground) opened the way for wagons and buggies to cross the river. (Courtesy Research Division of the Oklahoma Historical Society.)

An early view of Tulsa shows Main Street looking south. Three modes of transportation are apparent: Horse-drawn buggies and wagons, motor vehicles, and street cars. At right is the Oil Well Supply Company building, indicating the presence of the petroleum industry in Tulsa County. (Courtesy Mid-Continent Oil & Gas Association of Oklahoma.)

Dr. Fred S. Clinton, who with his friend Dr. J.C. Bland drilled Tulsa County's first successful oil well, practiced medicine in Red Fork. He was an ardent booster of the small town in its rivalry with Tulsa to determine which would benefit most from the rush to the area brought about by the drilling of the well. Within a few years, Clinton built a home in Tulsa. (Courtesy Tulsa Historical Society.)

In 1906, Dr. Fred S. Clinton and his wife, Jane Heard Clinton, moved from Red Fork to Tulsa. They lived in this large house at 502 South Cheyenne and soon became prominent community leaders and boosters of Tulsa. (Courtesy Research Division of the Oklahoma Historical Society.)

14

In another part of the Creek Nation, about 50 miles southeast of Tulsa, a few wells had been drilled near Muskogee in the 1890s, but they proved to be unproductive. In 1904, however, wells drilled in the Muskogee field produced as much as 500 barrels of oil each day. News of their success brought oilmen and speculators from Tulsa and other areas to drill for oil.

A view of oil wells and a primitive refinery at Muskogee is shown on this postcard. It was in Muskogee that the Oklahoma petroleum refining industry got its start before statehood. As additional fields were developed throughout Indian Territory, numerous other refineries would be built, including those in Tulsa.

Tulsa was not far behind Muskogee in obtaining a refinery. In 1907, the year in which Indian Territory was merged with Oklahoma Territory to form the state of Oklahoma, the Uncle Sam Refining Company opened a refinery in Tulsa. The Tulsa refinery was used mainly to process oil from the Osage Nation north of Tulsa in what is now called Osage County, the largest county in the state.

This postcard depicts the "shooting" of an oil well in the Nowata area. The process intended to increase the production from a well was often used in the Tulsa area and other oil fields. Whenever a drill reached a depth that indicated the presence of oil, it was the practice to drop a charge of nitroglycerine into the well to shatter the oil sand, thereby allowing the crude oil to flow more rapidly into the well.

Two

THEN CAME
GLENN POOL

In 1906, when this postcard was mailed from Tulsa, Indian Territory, the reverse side of a card was intended to be used only for an address. For that reason the message was written on the front, underneath the view of an oil field scene near Tulsa. The entire message was "Didn't know I was at Tulsa, did you? Write later," with no signature. The card showed a scene that was typical of the Glenn Pool, discovered a year earlier.

Robert Galbreath, who had drilled some wells at Red Fork, enlisted the financial support of Frank Chesley of Tulsa in drilling the well called the Ida Glenn No. 1, about 12 miles southwest of Tulsa. Drilling began in the fall of 1905 and continued through October and most of November with nothing to show for it. By the time it reached 1,400 feet, Galbreath and Chesley were discouraged, but decided to go down another 100 feet. Finally, at around 5 a.m. on November 22, the well blew in as a gusher that flowed high above the top of the derrick. The Glenn Pool was the first major oil field in Oklahoma, and Tulsa reaped the benefits from it. (Courtesy Tulsa Historical Society.)

Oklahoma is often called "The State That Oil Built," the title of a booklet published by the American Petroleum Institute in the early 1940s. After the Red Fork discovery, leasing and drilling continued in an effort to find other oil fields. It was in 1905 that dreams began to come true when the discovery well was drilled for the hugely profitable Glenn Pool. After that occurred, Tulsa became "The City That Oil Built" and what the API booklet called "the oilman's home town."

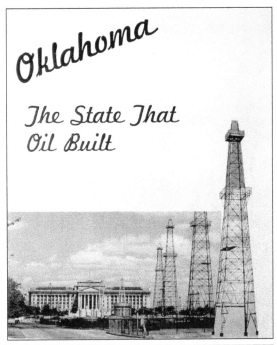

Oklahoma

The State That Oil Built

As the result of the discovery of the Glenn Pool, the town of Glenpool was created. Drilling took place throughout the area, but newspaper accounts and photographs usually referred to the "Glenn Pool, Tulsa, Okla.," as this early photograph inscription did. In recent decades, the population of Glenpool has grown considerably, and the town is now a prosperous suburb of Tulsa.

19

Oil derricks in the Glenn Pool extend as far as the eye can see in this early postcard. The caption on the card refers to the "Glen Pool Oil Fields, Tulsa, Okla." The spelling of Glen with only one "n" was quite common, and the correct spelling of the name for the town of Glenpool uses only one "n" instead of two, even though the pool was named for Ida B. Glenn, on whose lease the discovery well was drilled.

This postcard, published by the Tulsa Indian Trading Company, shows an oil tank farm in the Glenn Pool. Throughout the history of the oil field there have been large tank farms in which oil is stored before being transported to refineries in Oklahoma and other states.

The town of Kiefer sprang up almost overnight after the discovery well for the Glenn Pool was drilled in November 1905. This picture, taken in about 1907, shows a muddy road lined by businesses in the center of the town, southwest of Tulsa. (Courtesy Tulsa Historical Society.)

A postcard mailed from Kiefer in 1918 told a sad tale: "Will get thru here tomorrow unless something else turns up. Would you hold my mail till I find out where we will go? We had a big fire here yesterday, burned 42 rigs I think, 10 tanks and 6 houses. Will be glad when we get away from here." It was signed "Harry." His story of the oil fields was much different from the tranquil scene shown in this postcard.

The Frisco Railway yards at Kiefer were kept busy during the Glenn Pool oil boom. In the upper part of this photograph are dozens of oil derricks and a number of tanks. In highly productive fields such as those in the Glenn Pool, wells were drilled close together. In later years, the state of Oklahoma was in the forefront in enacting conservation rules that required more space between wells. Oklahoma also established regulations to prevent the waste of natural gas and oil and took the leadership role in bringing about the formation of the Interstate Oil Compact Commission, thereby assuring coordination with other oil producing states in the conservation of natural resources.

Glen Pool Oil Field   TULSA, Okla.

An oil tank and nearby derrick cast a perfect reflection in this lake of oil in the Glenn Pool field. Views such as this were frequently photographed for publication on the front of postcards and in newspapers and magazines of the period. The oil fields attracted workers from many other states, as evidenced by the fact that picture postcards were often sent home to relatives in such places as New Jersey, Connecticut, and California.

A VIEW OF GLENN POOL, TULSA, OKLA.

From the early days of the Glenn Pool, Tulsa became the center of the oil industry in eastern Oklahoma. Major oil companies established offices there, and many independents and small companies got their start in the city. Even though Tulsa enacted an ordinance prohibiting the drilling for oil within its city limits, the name of Tulsa was usually associated with the Glenn Pool, as on this postcard.

Lakes of oil in the Tulsa area varied in size. One of the lakes created for the overflow storage of oil measured five acres. Some people had the idea, after seeing a scene such as this one, that crude oil occurred in lake form, but the fact is that the oil was produced from underground sands that contained crude oil and/or natural gas.

Waite Phillips, a pioneer oil man who in later years would establish one of Tulsa's major art museums, is shown at far left in this 1907 photograph taken at a well site in Indian Territory, shortly before the territory became part of the new state of Oklahoma. Waite was then working for his brothers, Frank and L.E. Phillips, whose Phillips Brothers company would become Phillips Petroleum Company. (Courtesy Tulsa Historical Society.)

Brothers Frank (left) and L.E. Phillips (right) of Bartlesville, who later founded Phillips Petroleum Company, are shown in this photograph taken in Osage County in about 1903–1905. At center is baby nephew Philip Phillips, who grew up to become a member of the company's board of directors. A portion of north Tulsa is in the county, the largest county in the state. (Courtesy Tulsa City-County Library System.)

Five Phillips brothers pose for a photograph in Bartlesville in 1907. From left to right, they are as follows: Fred, Waite, Ed, L.E., and Frank. The two who became the most famous were Frank, who headed Phillips Petroleum Company for many years, and Waite, who became prominent in Tulsa as a philanthropist. The mansion he and his wife built became the world-renowned Philbrook Museum of Art. (Courtesy Tulsa Historical Society.)

LAKE OF OIL, GLENN POOL, TULSA, OKLA.

An earthen dam holds a supply of crude oil in the Glenn Pool near Tulsa. Numerous oil wells dot the horizon behind rows of storage tanks in this postcard scene published by the Tulsa Indian Trading Company. Scenes of overflow storage lakes such as this were apparent throughout the Glenn Pool area.

Oil Fields, with Sapulpa, Okla. in the distance

At Sapulpa in Creek County, about 10 miles southwest of Tulsa, the discovery well for the Sapulpa Field was drilled in 1909 as an extension of the Glenn Pool. This photograph shows the large number of producing wells in the field, which was sometimes referred to as the Pumpkin Center Field.

26

Earthen Oil Reservoir near Sapulpa, Okla.

It took a large amount of dirt and gravel to build an earthen reservoir of this size to hold some of the oil produced nearby. Shown in the background of this view from the Sapulpa field are oil derricks and oil storage tanks. This card was published by F.C. McClanahan of Sapulpa and printed in Germany.

Producing Oil Wells, near Sapulpa, Okla.

The tall derricks standing above oil producing wells in the Sapulpa Field reach high above the surrounding trees. As with other fields in the early days of oil production in Oklahoma, wells were drilled close together—a practice that was halted in later years when statewide rules required that wells be spaced farther apart for conservation reasons.

A thick cloud of black smoke is blown by the wind above the Sapulpa oil field in this photograph taken during the early days of oil production in the area. This fire, like so many others across the state, was caused by lightning that struck an oil tank. This picture was published by the *Sapulpa Democrat* newspaper.

A close view of an oil tank fire near Sapulpa shows the tremendous amount of smoke that poured from above the flame in this photograph. Enormous amounts of oil were destroyed by fire in the early days of oil production in northeastern Oklahoma. Most of the blazes were caused by lightning strikes during thunderstorms that occurred primarily during spring months.

One of Oklahoma's Oil Tank Farms, near Sapulpa, Okla.—4

More than three dozen storage tanks holding crude oil are lined up in perfect rows in this tank farm in the Sapulpa area southwest of Tulsa during the early 1900s. Many such tank farms were built throughout northeastern Oklahoma and other oil producing parts of the state.

In the Okmulgee area, about 38 miles south of Tulsa, oil was discovered in 1906, but the well's production was meager. In 1907, however, the Tulsa Fuel and Manufacturing Company drilled a well that produced 5,000 barrels a day. News of the discovery brought oilmen rushing to what became known as the Morris Pool. In this photograph, the town of Morris, established in 1903, is in the background.

The North Field in Okmulgee County became the scene of numerous derricks during the early 1900s. Drilling activity in Okmulgee County took place about 25 miles south of Glenpool. Most wells drilled in the county were from 1,000 to 2,000 feet deep. In addition to the Morris Pool, several other pools were discovered nearby at around the same time, but their production was marginal.

Flowing of Carter Well near Okmulgee, Okla.

A Carter Oil Company well flows above the top of the derrick near Okmulgee. Carter was a subsidiary of Standard Oil Company (New Jersey), which eventually became Exxon. The company for many years had a significant number of employees in its Carter Oil offices in Tulsa and in the Jersey Production Research Company in Tulsa.

Three

IMAGES OF PETROLEUM

Lease-holders proudly contemplate the surrounding oil field from a good vantage point near Okmulgee in about 1918. Wildcatters had a high percentage of success in Oklahoma from the earliest days of drilling through the 1910s and 1920s. Royalty owners prospered as they shared in the income that came from wells drilled on their land. (Courtesy Mid-Continent Oil & Gas Association of Oklahoma.)

An early refinery in Okmulgee seems minuscule in size compared with those of later years that have numerous towers and units that process crude oil into gasoline, heating oil, and other products. Okmulgee remained a refining center during most of the 20th century.

By 1917, there were five oil refineries in Okmulgee. The Okmulgee Refining and Producing Company plant processed only oil from the Okmulgee area. The refinery with the greatest capacity was owned by the Indiahoma Refining Company; it ran 3,500 barrels from Okmulgee, Cushing, and Kansas. The oldest Okmulgee refinery was built by Empire Refineries in 1907, and the other four were constructed between 1910 and 1917.

The Okmulgee Refining and Producing Company refinery in Okmulgee was built in 1916 and had a capacity of 1,000 barrels of crude oil per day. This photograph shows agitators, tanks, and an earthen pit. Agitators are mixing devices used to bring about contact between liquids or solutions of dissolved solids or to keep solids suspended in liquids. (Courtesy Tulsa City-County Library System.)

Among Oklahoma's many refineries was this one built in 1916 by the Sinclair Refining Company at Vinita, about 60 miles northeast of Tulsa. With a crude oil capacity of 10,000 barrels a day, it was one of the six largest refineries in the state in 1918, processing oil from the Osage and Garber fields.

In 1918, there were 67 operating refineries in Oklahoma, the largest of which was the Cosden & Company refinery built in 1912 in west Tulsa, just across the Arkansas River. Josh Cosden, head of the company, was one of the most popular of the big-name oilmen who made their wealth in the fields near Tulsa. His refinery had a capacity of 30,000 barrels a day and would eventually become the largest independent oil refinery in the world. Cosden, known as the "Prince of Petroleum," built Tulsa's first skyscraper and a showplace home with a tennis court and indoor swimming pool. But his lavish lifestyle ended when he went broke. He then made another fortune, but the Depression caused him to lose that. He died at the age of 59 in 1940. His refinery later underwent several name changes. After oil company mergers occurred, it would be known as the Mid-Continent, DX Sunray, Sun Oil Company, and Sunoco refinery.

Photographs of wooden derricks were popular subjects for postcards sold in Oklahoma long after the oil companies started using steel derricks. This photograph from the early 1900s was mailed from Tulsa to an addressee in Massachusetts. The writer described northeastern Oklahoma in 1937: "We rode out to oil well locations and refineries Monday, also to the Osage Indian town of Pawhuska. Everything is so different here—cities all new, country full of wells and mining properties."

Two men stand in front of a derrick at the corner where four leases meet near Tulsa. The sender of this card wrote to his son in Kansas City: "Here's a close-up showing in pretty good detail the 'rigs' and pumps. Four different owners come together right here."

Flowing Oil Well, Tulsa, Okla.—4

The height of the wooden derrick above the well from which oil spews, as shown in this classic photograph, can be measured against that of the two men entering the barn at left. The photograph was taken at a well site not far from Tulsa.

FOUR STAGES IN SHOOTING AN OIL WELL.
TULSA, OKLAHOMA.

Four stages involved in the "shooting" of an oil well in the Tulsa area are displayed in the photographs on this card. The "shooting" process starts with the dropping of a canister containing nitroglycerine into the well hole to shatter the oil-bearing sand in order to facilitate the flow of oil, such as that seen in various stages of eruption in these pictures.

36

Pond of Oil in Tulsa Oil Field, Tulsa, Okla.

A picturesque scene of trees, clouds, and a vast lake of oil in which an oil derrick is reflected provides a tranquil look at a portion of what this postcard refers to as the Tulsa Oil Field, but which most likely was the Glenn Pool field. Scenic postcards such as this proved popular with visitors to the state.

7353. A Gusher in the Glen Pool Oil Field, Tulsa, Okla.

The gusher in this Glenn Pool view is almost obscured by nearby trees and the heavy flow of oil that falls to the ground. The well erupted with crude oil that extended high above the trees. This picture is unusual in that it was taken in a forested area instead of one that had been cleared. An identical photograph was published on a postcard that said the well was near Okmulgee.

A man who signed this card as "Daddy" sent it to "Sonny Boy" in Kansas City in 1921, telling him about the risks involved in drilling for oil: "This is a good view of the oil fields. Some folks make a lot of money in oil, while others lose some. Funny stuff isn't it?"

Pond of Oil, near Tulsa, Okla.

Another card Daddy sent to Sonny Boy in 1921 points out, "All this that you see here that looks like water is crude oil. Isn't there some bunch of it?" The earthen dams surrounding the oil helped keep it under control. In the background are a field of derricks and storage tanks.

A freight yard filled with rows of pipe used in drilling for oil is the subject of this photograph, taken (as the card's caption says) at an oil field town near Tulsa. The town was probably Kiefer or Sapulpa, both of which were oil towns along the Frisco Railway line, which also goes through Tulsa.

Oil Field Scene, near Tulsa, Okla.—30

This scene of oil derricks along a river near Tulsa shows either the Arkansas River or the Cimarron, with several of the wells in the river itself and others along the outer banks. This same view of offshore oil operations was reprinted on postcards for many years.

A long train chugs through one of the oil fields near Tulsa. Beyond the tracks, numerous derricks and oil tanks extend far into the horizon, and in the foreground, a single derrick towers above the nearby trees. Trains and pipelines were the main modes of transportation for crude oil.

There is a look of disgust on the faces of three men as they view the problem brought about by a break in an oil pipeline near Tulsa in 1917. Two of the men, with tools in their hands, seem ready to tackle the problem, while the third man (perhaps a supervisor) stands with hands in his pockets.

This postcard provides a close up view of a crude oil storage tank in an oil field (probably the Glenn Pool) close to Tulsa. Other tanks, built close together, are interspersed with wells. Such pictures show the immensity of the oil activity that has taken place in the area.

Perhaps the five observers in this picture are owners proudly surveying their petroleum property near Tulsa, or they could be visitors or prospective investors hoping to learn more about oil production. In any event, they chose a perch that enabled them to oversee the landscape. Shown here are a drilling rig, oil well pumping unit, power, and receiving tanks.

Town lots in Jenks, a few miles southwest of Tulsa on the way to Glenpool, are shown in this photograph. The Midland Valley Railroad running through Jenks enlarged its facilities and installed loading racks there in order to provide for oil tank cars to carry oil from the Glenn Pool. Today, Jenks is one of the fastest growing suburbs of Tulsa. (Courtesy Tulsa City-County Library System.)

55,000 Barrel Oil Tank on Fire, near TULSA, Okla.

The smoke is so thick and black in this photograph of an oil tank fire near Tulsa that it obscures the view of the 55,000 barrel tank itself. A note on the front of the postcard indicates that the fire occurred on November 25, 1915.

Pools of oil were discovered in the early part of the 20th century in just about every town near Tulsa, including such places as Broken Arrow, Sand Springs, Bixby, and Mounds. As Tulsa has extended its city limits, most of these towns adjoin the boundaries of Tulsa. Here is a photograph of Well No. 1, drilled in the Mounds area by Sheppard Oil Corp. on its Mounds Lease. (Courtesy Tulsa City-County Library System.)

Although oil tank fires were not unusual in the oil fields of eastern Oklahoma, the flames and smoke often attracted nearby persons who owned cameras, resulting in many spectacular images that were used on postcards such as this one showing a 55,000 barrel tank on fire in the Glenn Pool field near Tulsa.

In this tranquil scene, a horse and wagon stand alongside a wooden derrick in the forefront of this Sapulpa oil field picture. Other oil derricks are scattered among the trees on the hills. (Courtesy Research Division of the Oklahoma Historical Society.)

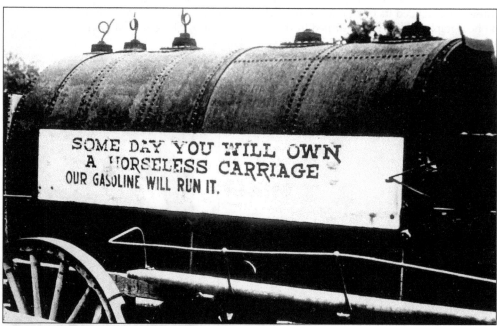

Horse-drawn tank wagons were used in the transportation of gasoline in the early days. This one, belonging to Standard Oil Company (New Jersey), bore a message that proved to be prophetic. The term "tank wagon" is still used in the wholesale marketing of gasoline. The modern-day tank truck provides safe, efficient, and economical transportation of gasoline. (Courtesy Tulsa City-County Library System.)

Four

THE OIL PATCH
EXPANDS

Cushing Oil Field Scene, Tulsa, Okla.—33
Showing Oil Activity in the Cimmaron River.

The Glenn Pool remained the biggest oil field in Oklahoma from 1905 until 1912, when a well drilled by Tom Slick and C.B. Shaffer discovered the Cushing field. The oil activity that followed in the Cushing-Drumright area included drilling alongside and in the Cimarron River near Drumright, about 40 miles west of Tulsa.

Flowing Well
near Cushing, Okla.

This photograph shows a flowing well that was typical of many that were drilled in the Cushing-Drumright area. Production in the field led to the aboveground storage of more than 1.75 billion barrels of unsold oil and resulted in the loss of valuable volatiles. Concern over the wasting of oil helped bring a maturity to the petroleum industry and an awareness of conservation needs.

Uncapped Oil Well in Cushing Field, near Tulsa, Okla.
Pitch black oil flowing from this well.

Black oil flows from this uncapped well, from which the derrick has been removed, in the Cushing field. Oil production in the Cushing-Drumright area, beginning about 40 miles west of Tulsa, was often referred to on postcards as "near Tulsa" because of Tulsa's prominence as the Oil Capital of the World. Many Tulsa oilmen drilled for oil in the highly productive field.

This photograph provides a close-up view of a ferry that carried passengers and horses and wagons across the Cimarron River near Drumright after the discovery of oil in the area. Since there were no bridges yet, the ferry owner was reputed to have "made a tidy fortune during the boom." Derricks show up faintly at right and at the top of the hill. (Courtesy Tulsa City-County Library System.)

A raging gas fire burns brightly at nighttime in the Cushing oil field. Before it was extinguished, it had consumed 70 million feet of gas. Seen by the light of the fire is a nearby derrick, and barely visible at far left is another well.

CUSHING REFINERY~ CUSHING. OKLA.

A railroad track runs in front of a refinery in Cushing. During the oil boom, the area became a major processing center with 23 refineries and numerous pipelines. Although the number of refineries eventually dwindled, Cushing became known as the "pipeline crossroads of the world," and a pipeline map of the area looks somewhat like a plate of spaghetti. A note on the card says, "This is sure wild and wooly around this city."

SINCLAIR OIL CO.-DRUMRIGHT.OKLA.

The Sinclair Oil Company plant at Drumright, about 40 miles west of Tulsa, was one of numerous gas and oil installations in the Cushing-Drumright area. Prominent Tulsa oilmen such as Harry Sinclair, James A. Chapman, and J. Paul Getty leased land and drilled for oil there, accumulating riches from the field.

At the Sinclair Pipe Line Company station in Hominy, employees pose for a picture in June 1924. Harry Sinclair, who made a million dollars in the Glenn Pool, established an integrated petroleum company in 1916 that consisted of oil production, refining, and transportation operations. (Courtesy Tulsa City-County Library System.)

The Cushing tank farm shown on this card was reputed to be the largest in the world, with a total of 573 tanks. Its capacity was 38,990,000 barrels of crude oil. In 1919, the Cushing-Drumright area accounted for 17 percent of the U.S. and three percent of the world production of oil. Its production peaked in May 1915 at 300,000 barrels per day. The field ranked as the nation's largest oil province from 1912 until 1920.

One of the most devastating and dramatic oil field disasters occurred in Drumright on the night of August 27, 1914, when thunderstorms moved into the area and lightning ignited a series of fires. Lakes of oil, exposed to the elements, caught on fire, as did storage tanks and wells. Shown here is a blazing tank alongside the Eastman Richards No. 1 well.

Among the disastrous fires caused by lightning in the Drumright area on August 27, 1914, was this one that attracted a number of spectators. Despite the tremendous amount of smoke that billowed above the fire, they stood or sat close by to watch the nighttime scene of destruction.

50

A flaming gas well at Dropright in the greater Cushing field casts a perfect reflection in this scene. When the town of Drumright came into being and mushroomed into an oil center, other towns or oil camps with copycat names were created. Unlike Drumright, however, Dropright, Damnright, Deadright, and others were short-lived, eventually disappearing as oil production declined.

An oil rig in the Cimarron River near Drumright looks like the Leaning Tower of Pisa as it begins to fall into the water in this photograph taken by the Electric Studio in Drumright sometime between 1915 and 1918. The collapse was probably caused by a rise in the river that was brought about by heavy rainfall in the area. (Courtesy Research Division of the Oklahoma Historical Society.)

The small town of Barnsdall (population now slightly more than 1,300) can boast of something that no other town or city can equal. It has the only Main Street oil well in America—not at the side of the street, but in the middle of it. Drilling was completed on March 16, 1914, at a depth of 1,771 feet. The sight is so unusual that visitors to Tulsa sometimes make a side trip to Barnsdall in neighboring Osage County, northwest of Tulsa, to photograph the unusual well that produced oil for many decades. Barnsdall is one of a number of Osage County towns that have played important roles in the history of the Oklahoma petroleum industry.

In the background of this photograph can be seen the Phillips Petroleum Company plant and laboratory that were built at Shidler in Osage County in 1925. A fractionating tower was added a year later. Phillips called its liquefied petroleum gas Philgas. (Courtesy Tulsa City-County Library System.)

Two of Oklahoma's most prominent oil leaders in the early days were Harry Sinclair, Sinclair Oil Company founder who lived in Tulsa many years, and Erle Halliburton of Duncan, founder of Halliburton Oil Well Cementing Company. At a drilling rig's floor in the Empire Field in southwest Oklahoma, Sinclair stands with his back to the camera. Halliburton (in dark suit) is at left. (Courtesy Research Division of the Oklahoma Historical Society.)

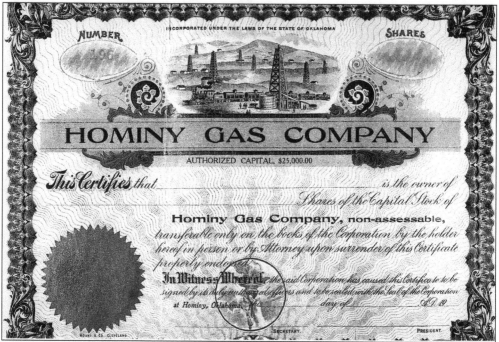

Many oil and/or gas companies that were incorporated in Oklahoma decorated their stock certificates with derricks, such as this one issued by the Hominy Gas Company in Osage County, northwest of Tulsa. Other companies' certificates were often adorned with pictures of refineries or other petroleum scenes. Some people collect such colorful certificates as oil industry souvenirs.

The Ingalls field in Payne County, between Stillwater and Tulsa, produced both oil and gas. Most of the activity in the area was between 1914 and 1916. The person sending this postcard back home to Illinois wrote, "We are still down where the oil is flowing free. We are having a great time."

Dallas D. Wertzberger, president of Wertzberger Derrick Company and a prominent Tulsan, is pictured at the wheel of his spacious 1914 model Cadillac touring car. He had driven a couple of his friends out to a rural area to show them an oil well. Visitors from outside the "oil patch" usually wanted to see producing wells such as the ones they had heard about. (Courtesy Tulsa Historical Society.)

Power equipment began to take much of the backbreaking work out of the chore of laying pipelines to carry oil and its products. As seen in this photograph, machines prepare a ditch and tractors hold the heavy pipe in place. A special wrapping apparatus is used to apply a layer of hot tar and a coating of impregnated asbestos felt. (Courtesy Tulsa City-County Library System.)

The Producers and Refiners Corporation built this pipeline pump station at Kiefer, near Tulsa. The same company was also a leading oil producer in the Burbank field in Osage County, with five wells completed in 1921. Many Tulsans were involved in the development of the Burbank area. (Courtesy Tulsa City-County Library System.)

A large crew is shown building steel oil tanks in this picture taken in Tulsa. Some of the men are busy using tools, but others seem to be resting while watching the others at work. During the boom days, great numbers of tanks were built in order to fill the need for crude oil storage facilities. (Courtesy Tulsa Historical Society.)

Five

TULSA BECOMES A METROPOLIS

As Tulsa grew, so did its reputation as the Oil Capital of the World. Drilling continued near the city and in other northeastern Oklahoma areas. Many Tulsa oil companies built headquarters and other buildings in the downtown area. New techniques brought about improvements in oil drilling and production. Steel derricks were being used instead of wooden ones, as shown in this photograph of oil fields near Tulsa, and rotary rigs were becoming commonplace.

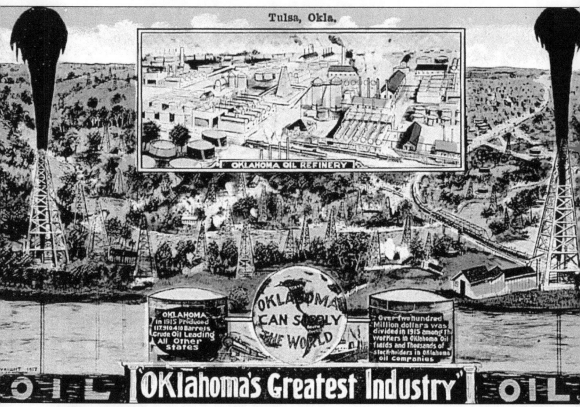

"Oklahoma Can Supply the World" is the boast made in the small globe at the bottom of this postcard that shows an oil field and two gushing wells. There was truth in the claim, as well as in the larger print proclaiming that oil is "Oklahoma's Greatest Industry." At the top of the card is the identification of "Tulsa, Okla.," below which is a picture of an oil refinery. More information about oil in Oklahoma is provided in the two oil tanks. One of them reads: "Oklahoma in 1915 produced 117,910,410 barrels crude oil leading all other states." In the barrel at right is the statement: "Over two hundred million dollars was divided in 1915 among the workers in Oklahoma oil fields and thousands of stock-holders in Oklahoma oil companies." It should be borne in mind that this card was published years before some of the largest Oklahoma oil discoveries took place—most notably the great Seminole field in 1926 and the giant Oklahoma City field in 1928.

58

When Oklahoma became a state in 1907, there were already several multi-story buildings in Tulsa. In 1912, the Fred S. Clinton office building was built by Dr. Clinton, one of the two medical doctors who had drilled the Red Fork discovery well. Standing eight stories high at Fourth Street and Boston Avenue, it was Tulsa's first fireproof building. (Courtesy Research Division of the Oklahoma Historical Society.)

The Sinclair Building at Fifth and Main in Tulsa was built by Harry F. Sinclair, one of the nation's most prominent oilmen, who started as an independent but eventually created an integrated oil company. The Sinclair company maintained a presence in Tulsa for many decades. It eventually merged with Atlantic Richfield. (Courtesy Research Division of the Oklahoma Historical Society.)

Perhaps the most famous building in Tulsa's early history was the Tulsa Hotel, built in 1912 on the northwest corner of Third Street and Cincinnati Avenue. It was much more than Oklahoma's finest hotel, a place that provided comfortable rooms and suites for out-of-towners to stay in during their visits to the Oil Capital. It soon became the center of the petroleum industry. Oil company executives and independent operators from Tulsa and other cities got together there to buy and sell leases and producing properties, arrange deals often worth millions of dollars, keep up with news affecting the industry, and discuss the world of petroleum in general. Often seen in the lobby were Harry Sinclair, who maintained a suite of offices in the hotel and came to Tulsa by train each day from his home in Independence, Kansas; J. Paul Getty, eventually the world's richest man; Josh Cosden, who made and lost two fortunes; and William G. Skelly, founder of Skelly Oil Company. Oil editors of prominent newspapers and periodicals set up desks in the lobby in order to file their stories as soon as petroleum-related news broke. (Courtesy Research Division of the Oklahoma Historical Society.)

Tulsa's first building with an elevator was the First National Bank building, completed in 1905 at Second and Main. It also had drinking fountains on each floor. Later, the bank moved into a larger building at Fourth and Main where it remained until 1950, when it moved to a new 20-story structure at Fifth and Boston. Many oilmen have served on the bank's board of directors. (Courtesy Research Division of the Oklahoma Historical Society.)

During the 1910s and early 1920s, many impressive buildings were constructed in Tulsa's downtown. They included oil company headquarters, banks, and hotels. Aptly named was the 10-story Petroleum Building at Fifth Street and Boulder Avenue. Many individual oil operators, geologists, engineers, consultants, and small oil companies had offices in the building. (Courtesy Research Division of the Oklahoma Historical Society.)

Some Tulsa oilmen, including Harry Sinclair, who needed to borrow large amounts of money to finance the expansion of their companies, finance leases, and provide funds for drilling ventures, decided to form their own bank. They bought the failing Farmers National Bank in 1910 and gave it the name of Exchange National Bank. (Courtesy Research Division of the Oklahoma Historical Society.)

What began as the Exchange National Bank underwent several name changes through the years after its formation. When it became the National Bank of Tulsa it was widely referred to as "The Oil Bank of America." In 1928, it built this skyscraper on Boston Avenue between Third and Fourth Streets. NBT was the first bank in the U.S. to have a petroleum engineering department. (Courtesy Research Division of the Oklahoma Historical Society.)

Three cars headed for Tulsa from Ohio are shown in this 1920 photograph. A sign on the nearest car proclaimed "Bound for the Oil Fields—We Stand the Gaff! 2000-Miles Overland from the White Motor Co., Cleveland to Skelly Oil Co. Tulsa, OK." Note the extra tires that were undoubtedly needed for the lengthy trip. (Courtesy Research Division of the Oklahoma Historical Society.)

One of the most striking additions to Tulsa's landscapes was the Philtower Building that opened in 1928 at the northeast corner of Fifth Street and Boston Avenue. The skyscraper was built by Waite Phillips, who also built other downtown structures including the Philcade, across from the Philtower, and the Beacon Building. (Courtesy Research Division of the Oklahoma Historical Society.)

A gathering of some of the most prominent citizens in the history of Tulsa, who had much to do with the growth and progress of the city, took place in 1926 at Stansbery Lake, owned by Lon R. Stansbery, not far from Tulsa. Among those shown in this photograph are Dr. Fred S. Clinton (second from the right) and Dr. J.C.W. Bland (far right), the pair who drilled the Red Fork discovery well. Others in the picture are: Arthur Antle, Harry Campbell, Admiral Henry B. Wilson, Prier Lee Price, J.W. Hall, Lon R. Stansbery, Robert D. Atkins, Fred Insull, and Colonel Patrick J. Hurley in the back row holding a little girl, Cecile Davis, a grand-niece of Dr. Clinton. Many years later, Cecile (then Cecile Richards) wrote a biography of Dr. Clinton's wife, Jane Heard Clinton. (Courtesy Tulsa Historical Society.)

A close look at the Mid-Continent Petroleum Corporation refinery (formerly the Cosden refinery) in Tulsa is provided in this image against the backdrop of the city's impressive downtown skyline. Long known for its skyscrapers, including the headquarters of oil companies, Tulsa in future years could boast of buildings 50 or more stories high.

Reflected in the Arkansas River that flows through Tulsa is one of the two refineries on the river's west bank. At dusk when the lights are shining and the sun is going down, such a scene is a beautiful sight. In addition to the Mid-Continent refinery, another prominent refinery was known for many years as the Texaco refinery and is now owned by Sinclair.

In the 1930s, oil field scenes such as this could be seen near Tulsa and in other parts of the state. In later years, petroleum drilling in Oklahoma was so widespread that oil and/or gas were produced in 72 of Oklahoma's 77 counties. In some instances, the amount was quite small, but in others vast quantities of petroleum were produced each year.

Since the early days of Tulsa's development, the growing city has been nationally recognized for its attractive downtown. Its buildings, taller than those of most cities its size and much cleaner than those in older cities, affirm Tulsa's reputation as one of America's most beautiful cities. This skyline photograph was taken in 1960. (Courtesy Research Division of the Oklahoma Historical Society.)

Six

The Grandest Oil Show

Tulsa's role as the Oil Capital of the World was reinforced on October 8–13, 1923, when the first International Petroleum Exposition, suggested by attorney Earl Sneed, was held downtown. It featured oil equipment displays, a parade, and crowning of "King Petroleo." In future years, the IPE would attract many more exhibits and international visitors. This view shows a nighttime panorama of derricks at one exposition. (Courtesy Tulsa Historical Society.)

A night view of an early International Petroleum Exposition and World Petroleum Congress shows lighted drilling rigs. By the time of the 1928 IPE, a dozen steel and wooden derricks were on display among the 258 exhibits. Twenty foreign nations were represented that year. Rotary drilling was featured, and emphasis was also put on aviation, following the transatlantic flight by Colonel Charles A. Lindbergh in the preceding year.

One of the most prominent Tulsa oil executives of all time was William G. Skelly, founder and chairman of the board of Skelly Oil Company, who in 1925 was named president of the International Petroleum Exposition. An indication of his popularity was the fact that he held the position for 32 years. During his tenure, the IPE became the largest trade exposition in the world. (Courtesy Tulsa Historical Society.)

It is unclear as to the year in which this postcard photograph of Tulsa's IPE was taken. The IPE moved from downtown to the area west of Peoria and Admiral Place in 1924 and then to its permanent location at the Tulsa Fairgrounds on East 21st Street in 1927. President Calvin Coolidge was present that year to set off a simulated gusher. During the early years, the IPE was usually held annually, but it was discontinued from 1931 until 1934 because of the Depression.

Crowds throng into the International Petroleum Exposition grounds in Tulsa during the 1930 show, held October 4–11. This card bears the emblem of Skelly Oil Company, which was founded by William G. Skelly, the IPE president. After the Depression, the IPE went to two-year intervals beginning in 1934 and extending through 1940. After that, they were held in 1948, 1953, 1959, 1966, 1971, 1976, and 1979.

An inscription on the reverse side of this postcard, depicting a flaming oil well owned by Skelly Oil Company, reads: "I have attended the 7th Annual International Petroleum Exposition at Tulsa and visited the Skelly Oil Company booth." Many of the IPE exhibitors handed out souvenirs to the public. So many people attended the expositions that many local citizens rented their homes to visitors when the IPE was held.

In 1938, the Oklahoma Petroleum Industries Committee displayed this car in front of the Mayo Hotel in Tulsa during the International Petroleum Exposition. Signs indicate how many different taxes were being paid by the motoring public. The Mayo Hotel was where many prominent visitors stayed during the IPE. (Courtesy City-County Library System.)

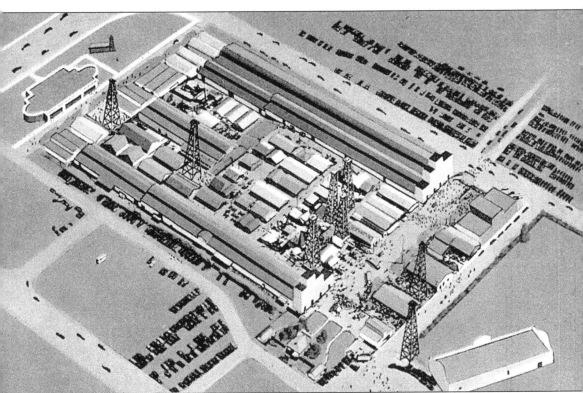

An airplane view of the 1940 International Petroleum Exposition, the last one before the United States entered World War II, is shown in this postcard that helped publicize the next IPE to be held on May 15–22 in 1948. The 1948 exposition, promoted as the "World's Fair of the Oil Industry in the Oil Capital of the World," observed the 25th anniversary of the IPE, which had its beginning in 1923 with 27 exhibits and 14,000 attendees. By contrast, the 1948 show had been enlarged to accommodate 800 exhibitors and an anticipated attendance of 200,000. The 1948 event included demonstrations of wartime and post-war petroleum equipment and processes for all phases of the petroleum industry. Displays in the Hall of Science featured "the world's most complete collection of technical and scientific exhibits."

Tentative plans had been made for the International Petroleum Exposition to be held again four years after the one in 1948, but the Korean War interfered. For that reason the IPE was postponed until 1953. Its run was lengthened to 10 days, from May 14 through 23, and an additional 35,000 square feet of outdoor exhibit space was made available. More foreign exhibitors participated than ever before. In order to alleviate the shortage of hotel rooms, arrangements were made to provide housing for visitors at more than a thousand private homes in Tulsa. One of the exhibit highlights was this drilling rig surrounded by a doughnut-shaped viewing area, which enabled visitors to sit or stand in air-conditioned comfort and watch the simulated drilling of a well.

Many people attending an International Petroleum Exposition for the first time were amazed at the immense size of equipment on display, such as drilling rigs and pump jacks that dwarfed bystanders. In this 1953 photograph, an American flag is suspended from a crane that reaches high into the sky. Nearly 1,500 exhibits represented all aspects of the petroleum industry that year. Many of the drilling rigs on display were capable of reaching record depths.

An early version of the Golden Driller that would later become the symbol of the International Petroleum Exposition and Tulsa itself was displayed at the 1953 IPE. In this version, the driller's left hand is upraised. A much larger image would eventually be created to stand in front of the main IPE building.

In 1959, the petroleum industry throughout the nation celebrated its centennial, commemorating the 100th anniversary of the drilling of the first oil well by Colonel Edwin L. Drake in Titusville, Pennsylvania. The 1959 International Petroleum Exposition participated in the celebration, prominently displaying the industry's centennial slogan: "Oil's First Century—Born in Freedom, Working for Progress."

Crowds at Tulsa's 1959 IPE far exceeded those of previous years, with more than 540,000 visitors attending. It was believed to have been the largest gathering of oilmen, more than 30,000, in the history of the industry. The most modern and sophisticated equipment used in exploration, production, refining, and transportation made its debut at the exposition.

A new version of the Golden Driller was introduced at the 1959 IPE; this one appeared to be climbing a drilling rig, with one hand holding onto the side of the rig and the other raised as if to wave to the crowd below. As time went by, the IPE was symbolized by the driller statue, which was a popular image that was often photographed by visitors.

The Tulsa-based *Oil & Gas Journal*, the leading petroleum trade magazine read around the globe, played a prominent role at each International Petroleum Exposition, providing information, news, and even a messenger service for the industry. In this 1959 photograph, a messenger in uniform stands by as a parade passes. At far right is W.A. (Bob) Roberts of Phillips Petroleum Company, who later became a Phillips executive vice president.

Tulsa received nationwide television coverage throughout the 1959 International Petroleum Exposition. An NBC news crew, assisted by personnel from Tulsa's KVOO-TV, provided news of IPE happenings each day on the "Today Show" with Dave Garroway. In this photograph, an NBC correspondent stands on a platform that is about to be hoisted high into the sky by a crane, in order to provide a panoramic view of the IPE grounds.

In connection with NBC's coverage of the IPE in Tulsa during the 1959 oil centennial, viewers of the network's "Today Show" could view the daily progress during the drilling of this well near Drummond, Oklahoma. Called "Big Dave No. 1" after show host Dave Garroway, the well drilled by Big Chief Drilling Company for Carl and Henry Gungoll of Enid proved to be a dry hole.

Brightly lighted drilling rigs at the 1959 IPE provided a spectacular nighttime scene. Although such rigs were among the largest displays of oil equipment, equally impressive were smaller exhibits that showed the newest technology and scientific achievements in petroleum exploration and production.

Dancing girls dressed in golden attire were a popular attraction at this exhibit sponsored by Mid-Continent Supply Company, a Kendavis Industry, at the 1959 IPE in Tulsa. The exhibit tied in with the company's Golden Driller statue that was displayed on the side of a drilling rig. Although the IPE was primarily aimed at equipment buyers from the industry, there were also "fun" exhibits that were of general interest.

In advance of the 1966 International Petroleum Exposition, Tulsa citizens voted overwhelmingly to build a new Tulsa Exposition Center at the fairgrounds to replace eight deteriorating buildings that previously housed many IPE exhibits. Commonly referred to as the "IPE Building," the new structure covered more than 10 acres and had a cable suspension roof that enabled exhibits to be seen without interior walls or posts hindering the view. The enthusiastic support of Tulsa civic leaders in arranging for a vote to finance such a structure put to rest, at least for awhile, suggestions that the IPE should be moved to another city. In this photograph, a crowd gathers for the opening ceremony at the 1966 IPE. Standing high is the newest version of the Golden Driller, a symbol of the IPE and Tulsa's major industry.

The keynote speaker at opening day ceremonies for the 1966 IPE on May 12 was Governor John Connally of Texas (shown at microphones). Also on the platform are IPE officials and other dignitaries, including Oklahoma Governor Henry Bellmon (at far right in first row). As indicated by cameras in the foreground, the event was widely covered by television stations and other media.

A view from the second level of the IPE Building shows huge displays of oil equipment provided by BJ Pumps, Borg-Warner, Lone Star Steel, and other companies at the 1966 oil exposition. Oil company representatives were able to learn about the newest techniques and equipment for drilling and production at the hundreds of indoor and outdoor exhibits.

In addition to petroleum representatives from other nations, many oilmen in the United States who had lived in Tulsa previously arranged to return to the city to attend the International Petroleum Exposition. Shown at left in this 1966 photograph is a former Tulsan, Robert Greenwood, who became executive director of the South Carolina Petroleum Council and went on to a staff position with the American Petroleum Institute in Washington, D.C.

Five years elapsed before the next International Petroleum Exposition was held in 1971. Improvements were made in the spacious IPE building, including better control of the indoor temperature. The building was packed with exhibits showing the most modern equipment and techniques that had been developed for the petroleum industry. A special effort was made to encourage more independent operators to attend.

In keeping with the growing nationwide interest in the environment, the 1971 IPE featured an Ecology Hall of Science that provided displays showing the petroleum industry's conservation practices. In addition, the Oklahoma Petroleum Council sponsored an Ecology Film Festival near the Ecology Hall, showing 24 films sponsored by individual companies and the American Petroleum Institute. Films were shown continuously each day in a 100-seat theater and were viewed by oil personnel as well as the public, which was limited to attending only the last four days of the IPE. The theater not only played a significant role in the industry's education effort, but it provided an opportunity for visitors to sit down for a half hour or so and rest after walking around the spacious IPE building and the outdoor grounds.

Petroleum industry educational materials were provided to IPE visitors in 1971 at a booth co-sponsored by the Oklahoma Petroleum Council and the American Petroleum Institute. In this photograph, Kathy Kemm, a student volunteer, assists at the exhibit. A poster bears an industry slogan: "A Country That Runs on Oil Can't Afford to Run Short."

The Golden Driller image was used on a Regal China container (left) of bourbon whiskey bottled by the James B. Beam Distilling Company in 1971. An inscription on the reverse states: "Tulsa: Oil Capital of the World. Host of the International Petroleum Exposition for the 15th time since 1923, this is the largest trade show ever. Hello Oklahoma!!" At right is a small model of the driller. The emblem was also the subject of a song by composer Martha Barrett: "I'm in Love with the Golden Driller."

In celebration of 1976 as the nation's bicentennial year, the International Petroleum Exposition had a theme of "Energy '76." The five-day show was shorter than usual, and it had been divided into two main sections. The largest one, for the petroleum industry itself, attracted 44,699 buyers, which exceeded the total at any previous IPE. A smaller section was intended for the public, which, however, could visit the industry portion by paying a small admission fee. Shown in this photograph is a large pump jack, decorated with stars in a patriotic motif, towering above the other indoor exhibits. The total value of equipment displayed at the IPE exceeded $2 billion. At far left in the photograph is the Bicentennial Energy Film Theater. At front and center, a family looks at a Cities Service Company display. The public section of the IPE was called the "Petroleum Panorama" and consisted of non-commercial educational exhibits sponsored by the industry and individual oil companies and service and supply firms. One of the most important exhibits was the "World of Petroleum," which showed oil activities throughout the world.

Donkey power is used to operate a threshing machine and a windmill in this exhibit recalling long-gone primitive times. The display featuring a live donkey was included in the "Petroleum Panorama" area of the 1976 International Petroleum Exposition. Shown at left in a dark suit is Sloan K. Childers, vice president of Phillips Petroleum Company.

More than 7,000 visitors to the 1976 International Petroleum Exposition viewed motion pictures about the petroleum industry and other forms of energy during the Bicentennial Energy Film Festival sponsored by the Oklahoma Petroleum Council. Featured were 34 movies from the United States, Canada, and Europe, believed to be the greatest variety of high quality films about energy ever shown in one place. The festival's theme was "Energy: Its Heritage and Horizons."

Standing beneath a massive oil well pump that reaches high above the second level of the IPE's 10.5-acre exposition building are visitors to the 18th Tulsa oil show, destined to be the last. It was centered primarily on onshore development and was given a lengthy name: "Energy '79: International Exposition and Congress: International Onshore Equipment and Service Oil Show." To avoid conflict with other oil shows being held around the world, it was scheduled for September 10–13, which made it the shortest IPE in history. Emphasizing the industry's onshore operations was a tacit admission that Houston's annual Offshore Technology Conference had detracted somewhat from Tulsa's prominence as the site of the industry's largest oil show. Under pressure from some company officials who thought the crowds of non-oil visitors interfered with their selling of equipment and services, the 1979 IPE, with the exception of the Hall of Science, was closed to the public. As in several past IPEs, the Oklahoma Petroleum Council sponsored an Energy Film Festival. It was open to the public throughout the four-day IPE.

An array of ceiling-high pipes and valves (called "Christmas trees" in the oil patch) were among the displays in the huge IPE building at the 1979 Tulsa oil show. A series of exhibits in the IPE Enhanced Recovery Hall of Science, open to the public, showed the latest methods of secondary and tertiary recovery of oil and gas. Such techniques provide additional supplies of petroleum from existing wells.

The 1979 IPE again featured drilling rigs in outdoor displays. When the show ended, plans were being made for another one in 1982. But after an analysis showed that fewer out-of-state oil people had attended than in the past, the IPE general manager suggested that future expositions be held in larger cities. In April 1980, the directors decided against another IPE and disbanded the sponsoring corporation, blaming dwindling finances and competition from other oil shows. Thus ended one of Tulsa's chief claims to the title of "Oil Capital of the World."

Seven

MARKERS AND RECOGNITION

The first oil historical marker sponsored by the Oklahoma Historical Society, State Highway Commission, and Oklahoma Petroleum Council honored the state's first commercial oil well, drilled in 1897. At the 1963 dedication near Bartlesville are, from left to right: Robert Newhouse, Tulsa; Muriel Wright, Oklahoma City; Nellie Johnstone (Mrs. Howard Cannon), for whom the well was named when she was a little girl; Elmer L. Fraker, Oklahoma City; and John Steiger, Bartlesville. (Courtesy Mid-Continent Oil & Gas Association of Oklahoma.)

Opposite, Top: Oklahoma Petroleum Council Historical Committee members help dedicate a marker commemorating the state's earliest refinery. The 1965 marker near Muskogee was sponsored by the Oklahoma Historical Society, OPC, and Highway Commission. They are, from left to right: Malcolm E. Rosser III, Halliburton, Duncan; unidentified; Paul Hedrick, retired oil editor, *Tulsa World*; Charles E. Cummings, Phillips Petroleum, Bartlesville; A.V. Bourque, Mid-Continent Oil & Gas Association, Tulsa; and John Steiger, Cities Service, Bartlesville. (Courtesy Mid-Continent Oil & Gas Association of Oklahoma.)

Opposite, Bottom: Four governors of oil-producing states are shown in Tulsa at an Interstate Oil Compact Commission meeting June 21, 1966, when a replica of a historical marker honoring the IOCC was presented by the Oklahoma Petroleum Council. They are, from left to right: John Steiger, OPC Historical Committee chairman; Governor Henry Bellmon, Oklahoma; Governor Clifford P. Hansen, Wyoming; Governor Paul B. Johnson, Mississippi; Governor John A. Love, Colorado; and W.A. Roberts, OPC president. (Courtesy Mid-Continent Oil & Gas Association of Oklahoma.)

Below: Tulsa's role as Oil Capital of the World was officially acknowledged in a granite monument placed in the Civic Center Plaza. The marker, level with the sidewalk, was dedicated October 7, 1969, during the Annual Meeting of the Oklahoma Petroleum Council. Oil leaders and city and county officials attended the ceremony. The text of the marker, sponsored by the Oklahoma Historical Society and OPC, traces the history of the "Oil Capital" title and points to Tulsa's importance as an oil center. They are, from left to right: John Steiger, OPC Historical Committee chairman; Wm. N. Pritchett, OPC president and Kerr-McGee vice president of marketing; Elmer L. Fraker, OHS administrative secretary; Mayor James M. Hewgley Jr.; Robert Newhouse, Tulsa county commissioner; Robert J. LaFortune, city commissioner; unidentified; and Anthony F. Keating, city commissioner. (Courtesy Mid-Continent Oil & Gas Association of Oklahoma.)

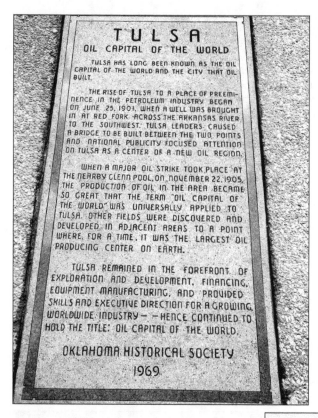

The history of Tulsa's "Oil Capital of the World" title, starting with the Glenn Pool oil strike and continuing through the 1960s, is cited in the 1969 granite marker in Tulsa's Civic Center Plaza. It calls attention to the fact that as of that date, the city was still the Oil Capital. (Courtesy Mid-Continent Oil & Gas Association of Oklahoma.)

A monument to the friendship of the petroleum industry and Osage Indians cited the role of the "Million Dollar Elm," under which oil lease sales were conducted. Participating in the dedication in Pawhuska on November 6, 1970, are, from left to right: Sylvester J. Tinker, principal chief of the Osage Indian Tribe, Pawhuska, and W.C. Bickel of Tulsa, vice president of the Oklahoma Petroleum Council, and vice president of the Gulf Oil Company-U.S. (Courtesy Mid-Continent Oil & Gas Association of Oklahoma.)

One of the most unusual monuments in Oklahoma pays tribute to the "Bond of Friendship" that existed between Osage Indian Chief Baconrind and Colonel E. Walters, who conducted lease sales under the "Million Dollar Elm." Including the pedestal on which the life-sized figures stand, the total height is more than 20 feet. The monument in the small town of Skedee was dedicated to Oklahoma by Colonel Walters in 1926.

A monument to the International Petroleum Exposition was dedicated at the Tulsa Exposition Center during the 1971 IPE. From left to right are the following: F. Randolph Yost, IPE president and president of Pan American Petroleum Corporation, Tulsa; and John Steiger, Oklahoma Petroleum Council Historical Committee chairman. The OPC and Oklahoma Historical Society co-sponsored the marker. (Courtesy Mid-Continent Oil & Gas Association of Oklahoma.)

The first gas-processing plant west of the Mississippi River was the subject of a historical monument sponsored by the Oklahoma Historical Society and the Oklahoma Petroleum Council in 1972. Dedication of the granite marker, eighth in a series of oil historical monuments sponsored by the two groups, took place south of Tulsa on June 15. From left to right are the following: (kneeling) John Steiger of Cities Service Oil Company, Tulsa, and chairman of the Council's Historical Committee; G.R. Brainard Jr., Atlantic Richfield Company, Tulsa, and Council president; Dr. V.R. Easterling, executive director, Oklahoma Historical Society, Oklahoma City; and Millard Hipple, Coastal States Gas Producing Company, Corpus Christi, Texas, and president of the Natural Gas Processors Association. The monument stands on the highway right-of-way at the intersection of U.S. Highway 75 and 141st Street in Glenpool. (Courtesy Mid-Continent Oil & Gas Association of Oklahoma.)

It was a chilly November day in 1972 when a marker honoring the importance of the Glenn Pool was unveiled near the discovery well site. Shown speaking is G.R. Brainard Jr., Atlantic Richfield Company, Tulsa and Oklahoma Petroleum Council president. Fourth from the left on the platform is Frank Galbreath, son of Robert Galbreath, who with Frank Chesley drilled the well that started Tulsa on its way to being the Oil Capital of the World.

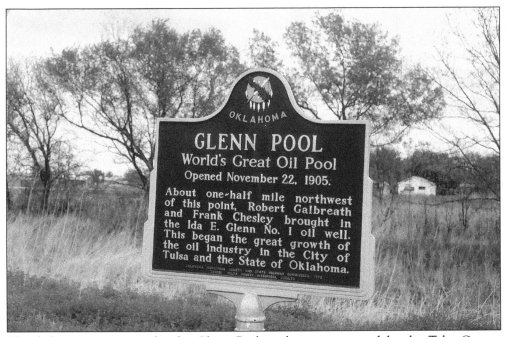

The dedication ceremony for the Glenn Pool marker was arranged by the Tulsa County Historical Society, which sponsored the marker along with the Oklahoma Historical Society and State Highway Commission. It was placed in Glenpool at the intersection of U.S. Highway 75 and 141st Street, next to the monument honoring the first gas-processing plant west of the Mississippi River.

Governor David L. Boren and two prominent Tulsa oil executives took part in celebrating the nation's bicentennial in 1976 with the dedication of a monument honoring Oklahoma's oil pioneers. The marker was placed on the grounds of the Oklahoma Historical Society in Oklahoma City, near a display of historic oil equipment. Pictured from left to right are: Jack Wettengel, executive director of the OHS, Oklahoma City; Wayne E. Swearingen, Swearingen Management Associates, Tulsa and chairman of Oklahoma Energy Awareness and Conservation Month (proclaimed by the governor); D.W. Calvert, president of the Oklahoma Petroleum Council and executive vice president of the Williams Companies, Tulsa; Mrs. Gladys Warren of Oklahoma City, chairman-director of the American Revolution Bicentennial Authority of Oklahoma; and Governor Boren. The text of the marker, co-sponsored by OHS and the OPC, stated that "Oklahoma's rise to prominence as a leading producer of oil, natural gas and refined products can be attributed in great measure to the determination and hardy spirit of its pioneers in the industry."

Robert V. Sellers of Tulsa (third from the right), chairman of the board, Cities Service Company, was the main speaker at a Chamber of Commerce luncheon in Bartlesville preceding the dedication of a monument paying tribute to the Bartlesville Energy Technology Center. At the unveiling on October 27, 1978, attendees were, from left to right: John Steiger, Tulsa consultant and Oklahoma Petroleum Council Historical Committee chairman; J.L. Jennings, Bartlesville Area Chamber of Commerce president; Dr. Warren L. Jensen, OPC president and vice president of Continental Oil Company, Ponca City; Robert V. Sellers; John S. Ball, Bartlesville, retired director of the center; and Jack Wettengel, executive director, Oklahoma Historical Society, Oklahoma City. The OHS and OPC co-sponsored the monument, which points out that petroleum technology in the United States began in Bartlesville March 28, 1918, when the U.S. government chose the city for the Petroleum Experiment Station, later known as the Energy Technology Center. (Courtesy Mid-Continent Oil & Gas Association of Oklahoma.)

Cushing was the site of a granite monument dedicated on the grounds of City Hall on December 12, 1979. The 15th in a series of historical markers co-sponsored by the Oklahoma Historical Society and the Oklahoma Petroleum Council, it cited the significance of the Cushing field and oil in the Cushing-Drumright area. The field ranked as the nation's largest oil province for eight years. Cushing is still known as the "pipeline crossroads of the world."

Local residents gather at the Bigheart Historical Museum in Barnsdall in 1981 for the dedication of a historical marker honoring the "Patriarch Petrochemical Plant of the Southwest." Manufacture of chemicals from petroleum had its beginning in the Southwest in 1926 at the Tallant gas processing plant three miles north. The monument was co-sponsored by the Oklahoma Historical Society and Oklahoma Petroleum Council.

A cube-shaped monument in the River Parks area at 41st and Riverside Drive in Tulsa shows the widespread oil and gas producing areas of Tulsa County. The marker was placed there for the people of Tulsa by the Tulsa Geological Society in recognition of the significance of petroleum to the Tulsa area and the state.

Joseph A. LaFortune of Tulsa was honored in 1975 with the Outstanding Oklahoma Oil Man Award from the Oklahoma Petroleum Council. Accepting for the honoree, who had died earlier that year, was his son, Tulsa Mayor Robert J. LaFortune (center), at the OPC Annual Meeting in October. George P. Bunn Sr. (left), retired Phillips Petroleum Company executive, Tulsa, presented the award. At right is Sloan K. Childers of Phillips, Bartlesville, OPC president. (Courtesy Oklahoma Petroleum Council.)

Six recipients of the Oklahoma Petroleum Council's Outstanding Oklahoma Oil Man Award were on hand at the Annual Meeting of the Council on October 10, 1978. Honored for his service to the petroleum industry and to Oklahoma was the 1978 winner, Jack H. Abernathy (holding award), vice chairman of Entex, Inc., Oklahoma City and Houston. Referred to as the "Oil Man of the Year Award," it was regarded as the highest honor bestowed upon an oil leader by the Oklahoma petroleum industry. Previous winners shown are, from left to right: W.W. Keeler (1971), retired chairman of the board, Phillips Petroleum Company, Bartlesville; Dean A. McGee (1970), chairman of the board of Kerr-McGee Corporation, Oklahoma City; John E. Kirkpatrick (1974), founder of Kirkpatrick Oil Company, Oklahoma City; P.C. Lauinger (1969), chairman of the board, Petroleum Publishing Company, Tulsa; and Wm. T. Payne (1966), president of Payne Petroleum Corporation and Payne, Inc., Oklahoma City, who was a founder of Tulsa-based Helmerich and Payne. Abernathy was the 18th oil leader to receive the annual award. (Courtesy Mid-Continent Oil & Gas Association of Oklahoma.)

Two oil executives who later became Outstanding Oklahoma Oil Man Award recipients are shown in 1955 at the time of the merger of Sunray Oil Company and Mid-Continent Petroleum Corporation. From left to right are Tulsans Robert W. McDowell, Mid-Continent president; Otis McClintock, First National Bank; and Clarence H. Wright, Sunray chairman. The merged company became Sunray DX Oil Company. Wright received the prestigious award in 1964 and McDowell in 1977. (Courtesy Tulsa Historical Society.)

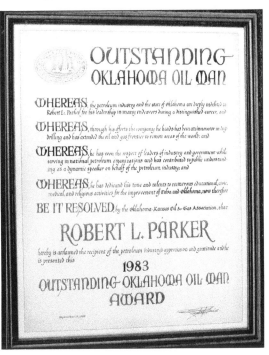

Each Outstanding Oklahoma Oil Man Award winner received a certificate such as this one awarded in 1983 to Tulsan Robert L. Parker Sr., Parker Drilling Co. chairman and CEO. Other Tulsa winners included: W.K. Warren (1967), Warren Petroleum Corporation founder; Davis D. Bovaird (1973), Bovaird Supply Company chairman; Henry Zarrow (1981), Sooner Pipe & Supply Company founder; John H. Williams (1982), the Williams Companies chairman; and Charles E. Thornton (1985), Reading & Bates Corporation president.

Recipients of Distinguished Service Awards from the Oklahoma Petroleum Council in 1980 are shown at the OPC Annual Meeting in Oklahoma City. M.R. Waller, Amoco Production Company, Tulsa and chairman of the Awards Committee, presented the plaques. From left to right are as follows: Waller; Wayne E. Anderson, Phillips Petroleum Company, Tulsa, accepting an award for H.F. Kinkead, Watts Oil Company, McAlester; C.L. Bowerman, Phillips, Bartlesville; R.D. Phillips, Charter Oil Company, Tulsa; J.J. O'Connell, Shell Oil Company, Tulsa; Paul W. Matthews, Highway Users Federation, Oklahoma City; and Robert Flaherty, ARCO Oil and Gas Company, Tulsa. Winners unable to attend were D.W. Calvert, the Williams Companies, Tulsa, and Walt Radmilovich, Oklahoma Natural Gas Company, Tulsa. The awards and similar plaques presented in other years recognized the recipients' leadership in the industry's education and information programs. (Courtesy Oklahoma Petroleum Council.)

Eight

THE LATER YEARS

Some of the many brand names of petroleum companies that have marketed gasoline and other products in Tulsa are depicted in these logos. Most of the companies represented have had marketing offices in Tulsa, and some have also had exploration and production headquarters or division or district offices in the city. Tulsa has also been the headquarters of numerous drilling and oil service and supply companies. (Courtesy Stokely Advertising of Tulsa.)

Visitors arriving at the Tulsa International Airport can see what undoubtedly is the largest and most impressive petroleum industry mural ever painted. The *Petroleum Panorama*, measuring 56 by 13 feet, was created in Tulsa by Delbert L. Jackson in 1966 and shipped to Washington, D.C., where it was displayed for years in the Smithsonian Institution Hall of Petroleum. This section of the polymer tempura painting depicts exploration and drilling methods in about 1966.

Of the 33 persons shown in the mural, 22 were Tulsa oil executives who posed for Jackson, a staff illustrator for Pan American Petroleum Corporation. This portion portrays crude oil production, refining and pipeline operations. In 1998, the city of Tulsa acquired the painting with the help of Gilcrease Museum and installed it at the airport through the generosity of the Amoco Foundation and the Helmerich Foundation. Jackson died in 1982.

Helmerich & Payne, Inc., with headquarters in Tulsa, used this giant rig to drill the Rumberger No. 5 well at a depth of 24,002 feet for Shell Oil Company about five miles south of Elk City in western Oklahoma. At the time it was completed, it ranked as Oklahoma's deepest and the world's second deepest oil well. Some drilling companies in Tulsa have moved to Houston or other cities, but Helmerich & Payne continues to make its home in Tulsa.

Beginning in 1947, Service Drilling Co.'s portable Rig No. 11 drilled 1.3 million feet of wells in the search for oil and gas. The rig was retired some years ago, but in 2002, Sherman Smith, chairman and chief executive of the Tulsa-based company, donated it to the Oklahoma Historical Society for display on the grounds of the OHS's new History Center in Oklahoma City. The exhibit also includes two other rigs and other oil equipment.

One of the leading manufacturers of drilling rigs, including the one shown in this photograph, has been the Lee C. Moore Company in Tulsa. The use of portable rigs made it possible to move from one location to another without building a derrick each time a well was drilled. Tulsa has been the home base for many of the world's largest drilling companies, as well as other service and supply firms. (Courtesy Tulsa City-County Library System.)

The fact that the *Oil & Gas Journal* is published in Tulsa has provided a good reason for the city to call itself the Oil Capital of the World. The magazine, read by oil people throughout the world and often referred to as "the big yellow book" or "the oil man's bible," is still published by PennWell at this 15th and Sheridan location in Tulsa, but its editorial offices are now in Houston.

Although Tulsa no longer is called the Oil Capital of the World, it remains the international headquarters for some of the industry's leading petroleum associations and scientific societies. Largest is the American Association of Petroleum Geologists, an international organization founded in Tulsa in 1917. It has a membership of 31,000 in 118 nations. The twin towers of its headquarters on South Boulder are shown in this architect's drawing. (Courtesy American Association of Petroleum Geologists.)

Much of the growth of the American Association of Petroleum Geologists can be attributed to the leadership of Fred A. Dix, executive director from 1973 to 1996. Dix, a geologist, is shown in the AAPG office with a display of rock cross-sections. The AAPG publishes the *AAPG Bulletin*, a scientific monthly, and *Explorer*, a four-color monthly newspaper for non-scientists. (Courtesy American Association of Petroleum Geologists.)

The Geophysical Resource Center of the Society of Exploration Geophysicists on South Yale in Tulsa is shown before it was occupied in 1985. The SEG business office is on the fifth floor and other floors are rented to businesses. The lobby houses the Geoscience Center consisting of a museum and educational facility. The SEG has about 20,000 members in more than 100 countries, with more members in other nations than in the United States and Canada. (Courtesy Society of Exploration Geophysicists.)

Three top staff members of the Society of Exploration Geophysicists are shown in this 1976 photograph. Seated is Howard R. Breck, SEG executive secretary (before the title of executive director was used). Standing are David Yowell (left), assistant executive secretary, and John Hyden (right), business administrator (before being named executive director in 1979). The SEG publishes *Geophysics*, a journal, and *The Leading Edge*, a monthly magazine. (Courtesy Society of Exploration Geophysicists.)

The Petroleum Equipment Institute was organized in Louisville in 1951 and opened its headquarters in Tulsa the same year. Shown at the fifth annual meeting are Ralph M. Lord (left), Wyoming Pump Service, Casper, and Howard Upton (right), executive vice president, secretary and general counsel from the time of its founding until his retirement in 1987. The PEI membership has grown to 1,643 companies in all 50 states and 81 countries. (Courtesy Petroleum Equipment Institute.)

Headquarters for the Petroleum Equipment Institute, originally known as the National Association of Oil Equipment Jobbers, is in this building on East 69th Street in Tulsa. PEI members manufacture, distribute, and service petroleum marketing and liquid handling equipment. Publications include the *Tulsaletter* and an equipment directory and technical and safety manuals. PEI sponsors an annual convention and a world trade exposition.

Ronald E. Cannon (shown here) served as executive director of the Gas Processors Association from 1957 until 1992 and was also secretary and assistant treasurer of the Gas Processors Suppliers Association, both of which have their headquarters in Tulsa. GPA has 100 corporate members: producers, processors, marketers, and transporters of natural gas liquids. It was organized in Tulsa in 1921 as the Association of Natural gas Manufacturers. (Courtesy Gas Processors Association.)

The longtime secretary of the Gas Processors Association until his retirement in 1986 was Carl B. Sutton. Both he and Ron Cannon are engineers and winners of the industry's prestigious Hanlon award. The GPA represents 90 percent of the nation's production of gas liquids and has three international chapters. It changed names twice before adopting its present name in 1974. (Courtesy Gas Processors Association.)

Deam Sims (at right), a consultant to the Tulsa-based International Society of the Energy Advocates, is presented a bust of himself in 1989 in appreciation of his service to the society since 1974 when he was one of its founders. Presenting the award is Ed Heminger, publisher of the *Courier* (Findlay, Ohio). Energy Advocates members, mostly oil executives, have traveled the nation to talk with audiences about U.S. energy issues. (Courtesy Energy Advocates.)

Energy Advocates from Tulsa participate in a panel discussion at a meeting of the National Press Club in Washington, D.C. Panel moderator Clyde W. LaMotte (left) of Washington, D.C. is pictured with energy company executives Howard Cowan and Ben G. Henneke Jr., both Tulsans. The more than 300 members of the Energy Advocates have communicated with the public and the media on many topics of current interest. (Courtesy Energy Advocates.)

Beginning in the late 1940s, the petroleum industry launched a public relations program to provide information about the industry. Cities and communities throughout Oklahoma joined in the effort, which included the observance of Oil Progress Week each October. This photograph shows oil people and civic leaders at a Chamber of Commerce luncheon during Oil Progress Week in Tulsa in the early 1950s.

Women employees of oil and related companies became good will ambassadors for the petroleum industry through the Desk and Derrick Club and the Oil Information Committee of the American Petroleum Institute during the 1950s. This photograph shows a group of Desk and Derrick women in Tulsa making plans for their participation in Oil Progress Week. The club also sponsors educational programs for members throughout each year.

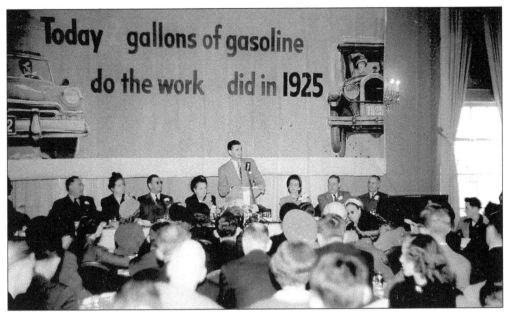

Progress of the oil industry in providing efficient motor fuels is pointed out on the banner that adorned the hotel ballroom in which this group gathered in the 1950s. The occasion was the "Oil Man and Woman for a Day" luncheon sponsored for high school students by the Tulsa Chamber of Commerce oil committee during Oil Progress Week. Each student spent the day with executives and employees of a sponsoring oil or service company, learning about their work.

A member of the Desk and Derrick Club of Tulsa (left) and Don Turner of National Tank Company, Tulsa, are shown at a booth sponsored by the American Petroleum Institute during an oil centennial celebration in Tulsa in 1959. Turner served as chairman of a petroleum information committee of the Tulsa Chamber of Commerce and was active in the API's Oil Information Committee.

The Oklahoma Petroleum Council, with headquarters in Tulsa, was formed in 1958 as a successor to the API Oil Information Committee. Beginning in the 1960s, it sponsored exhibits at annual conventions of the Oklahoma Education Association. Teachers at this 1964 convention ordered large quantities of educational materials about the oil industry for use in science and social studies classes.

Delaware Governor Pierre S. du Pont visits with oil executives at the Oklahoma Petroleum Council's 1979 Annual Meeting in Tulsa. Shown are, from left: Dr. Warren L. Jensen, OPC president and Conoco Inc. vice president, Ponca City; Charles A. Neal Jr., Chas. A. Neal & Company, Miami, and OPC vice president; Du Pont; Jack D. Jones, Getty Refining & Marketing Company president, Tulsa; and J.M. Tharp Jr., Getty Oil Company vice president, Tulsa.

Nine

A LEGACY OF
PETROLEUM

The Gilcrease Museum in Tulsa is a major attraction that draws visitors from all over the world. It was founded by Thomas Gilcrease, who made his fortune in oil at Glenn Pool and devoted his life to collecting art of the American West. Shown here in 1988, the museum on the northwest side of Tulsa houses his collection of paintings, artifacts, and historic documents. The building and Gilcrease home next door were built of native stone from the property.

When this postcard was issued, it proclaimed the Gilcrease Museum to be the most outstanding of its kind in the world, pointing out that it featured 10,000 paintings and sculptures depicting the western expansion of the United States. Also included at Gilcrease are documents and letters dating back to the earliest days of American discovery.

Thomas Gilcrease sits beneath a portrait of his daughter, Des Cygne, in his home on the grounds of the Gilcrease Museum in Tulsa. The house was built by Native American labor using stones taken from the property. Gilcrease befriended leading Indian artists, such as Woody Crumbo, Acee Blue Eagle, and Willard Stone, all of whose works are included in the museum along with paintings and sculptures by such artists as Frederic Remington and Charles Russell. (Courtesy Tulsa Historical Society.)

Waite Phillips, a Tulsa oilman who made his fortune as an independent operator in the Okmulgee field, built several of Tulsa's most majestic office buildings and a palatial home that is now the Philbrook Museum of Art. He is shown here in the mid-1930s in his office in the Philtower Building at Fifth Street and Boston Avenue. (Courtesy Tulsa Historical Society.)

Villa Philbrook was built by Waite Phillips in 1927 on 23 acres of wooded land at 2727 South Rockford Road. After living there with his family for some years, Phillips donated the mansion and grounds to the city for use as an art center. Shown here is the spacious garden area at the rear of the 72-room house, which became a museum in 1939. Several large additions have been made since then at what is now known as the Philbrook Museum of Art.

Beacon Building
donated by Waite Phillips
an endowment to the

To make certain that Philbrook could continue to operate as a museum, Waite Phillips in 1939 donated the Beacon Building in Tulsa as an endowment to support the art center. He also gave the Boy Scouts his huge Philmont Ranch in New Mexico and arranged for income from space rental in the Philtower Building to pay for the ranch upkeep. He made numerous other major contributions to Tulsa before moving to Los Angeles. (Courtesy Tulsa Historical Society.)

Many Tulsa oilmen have contributed large sums to the University of Tulsa. As a former TU dean said, "You can look in any direction on our campus and you will see a building that is here because of the generosity of someone in the oil industry." An example is the McFarlin Library, funds for which were donated by Robert M. McFarlin. His oil business partner, James M. Chapman, left his entire estate to a trust, naming TU as the main beneficiary.

William G. Skelly, founder of Skelly Oil Company, was one of Tulsa's foremost civic leaders and philanthropists. He owned radio station KVOO, was co-owner of television station KVOO-TV, and founded Spartan Aircraft Company and the Spartan School of Aeronautics, both in Tulsa. In this photograph, he is shown with a Spartan airplane and an unidentified pilot. Skelly was often called "Mr. Tulsa." (Courtesy Tulsa Historical Society.)

Skelly Stadium on East 11th Street in Tulsa, the location of University of Tulsa football games, was named for William G. Skelly, whose donation and leadership made the stadium a reality in 1929. Skelly also donated funds for the university's radio station KWGS. Other Tulsa landmarks named after him are Skelly Drive (a portion of Interstate 44) and Skelly Elementary School. Skelly was president of the International Petroleum Exposition for 32 years.

Natalie and William K. Warren (third and fourth from the left) are shown with two unidentified couples as they prepare for an airplane trip. Warren was the founder of Warren Petroleum Corporation in Tulsa, president of the International Petroleum Exposition for 10 years, and the winner of the 1967 Outstanding Oklahoma Oil Man Award. He and his wife created the charitable Warren Foundation in 1945. (Courtesy Tulsa Historical Society.)

St. Francis Hospital was built on a 26-acre hill at 61st and Yale Avenue by William K. and Natalie Warren through the Warren Foundation. Dedicated in 1960, it was donated to the Sister Adorers of the Most Precious Blood. At a cost of $8 million, it was then the largest single gift ever made by individuals to a Catholic order. The foundation later provided funds for other medical buildings and a new Montereau in Warren Woods retirement center.

This view of a ball field at LaFortune County Park, extending east of Yale Avenue from 51st Street to 61st Street, shows the St. Francis Medical Center in the background. Joseph A. LaFortune Sr., who donated land for the park, was the former vice chairman of Warren Petroleum Corporation, headed by W.K. Warren, who created the Warren Medical Center. Their gifts to Tulsa are among the most visible examples of charitable donations to benefit Tulsans.

The LaFortune name is among the most prominent in Tulsa, starting with oilman Joseph A. LaFortune Sr. (shown here), whose interest in community improvement led him to provide funds for LaFortune County Park and Golf Course on land he donated to the county. His son, Robert J. LaFortune, an oil operator, became mayor of Tulsa, and a grandson, Bill LaFortune, was later elected to the same position. (Courtesy Oklahoma Petroleum Council.)

The 16-story Petroleum Club Building at Sixth Street and Boulder Avenue is one of two downtown clubs, the other being the Summit Club, where many leaders of the oil industry gather. Primarily a business and social club, the Petroleum Club built this addition to the Tulsa skyline in 1962. During the 1960s and 1970s, the club had a waiting list of hundreds of applicants for membership.

Many Tulsa buildings in which oil companies had offices or headquarters have been adapted for other purposes now that the companies have moved from the city, merged with other companies, or reduced the number of Tulsa employees. An example is the former headquarters of Amerada Petroleum Corporation (later known as Amerada Hess), which is now occupied by Community Care of Oklahoma.

Among the most prominent oilmen in Tulsa's history was Walter H. Helmerich, co-founder and chairman of Helmerich & Payne, Inc., which has had its headquarters in Tulsa since 1924. Under his leadership, the company became one of the nation's foremost drilling companies. He also established the Helmerich Foundation and began a tradition of philanthropy that has been continued by his family. (Courtesy Helmerich & Payne, Inc.)

Walter Helmerich III, chairman of the board of Helmerich & Payne, expanded its drilling operations worldwide and developed real estate interests, including Tulsa's upscale Utica Square. The Helmerich Foundation has donated funds for numerous causes, including a park, museums, and a library and women's health hospital named for his wife, Peggy, a civic leader. The Tulsa City-County Library's Peggy V. Helmerich award is one of the nation's most prestigious literary awards. (Courtesy Helmerich & Payne, Inc.)

One of the best examples of the generosity of Tulsa oil leaders is Henry Zarrow, founder of Sooner Pipe & Supply Company. After rising to prominence from humble beginnings, he has contributed large sums to public education, libraries, a day center for the homeless, plus many other charities and cultural causes. Lovingly called "Mr. Henry," he credits his late wife Anne for her partnership in philanthropy. (Courtesy Zarrow Family Office, L.L.C.)

Jack Zarrow, former president of Bigheart Pipe Line Corporation, and his wife Maxine have been involved with Gilcrease Museum for 35 years. In the view of a former Gilcrease executive director, Jack Zarrow, younger brother of Henry Zarrow, "epitomizes the spirit of giving." The couple's leadership and financial contributions have benefited Gilcrease and many other Tulsa charitable, cultural, and civic organizations. (Courtesy Zarrow Family Office, L.L.C.)

The sprawling complex of buildings that was formerly the Research Center for Amoco Production Company in Tulsa now belongs to the University of Oklahoma. Situated in a campus-like setting at 41st Street and Yale Avenue, it is the Schusterman Center, named for the late Charles Schusterman, whose financial support made it possible for the university to acquire the property. Amoco had used it for research into new techniques for oil exploration and production.

One of Tulsa's most impressive buildings is the Mabee Center on the campus of Oral Roberts University on South Lewis Avenue. The arena is the site of ORU basketball games, high school graduation ceremonies, concerts, religious services, and a wide variety of other activities. It is named for oilman John Mabee, whose contributions to education and other worthwhile causes have been of immense value to Tulsans.

Sinclair Oil & Gas Company built this structure at 11th and Boston Avenue for its regional exploration and production headquarters. A portion of the building was set aside for use by Tulsa Community College. Sinclair, which had been an important part of the Tulsa oil industry, later merged with Atlantic Richfield Company. After ARCO's departure from Tulsa, the college became the sole occupant of the building.

Some of Tulsa's leading oilmen have served in city, state, and national elected positions. One of the most prominent was Dewey F. Bartlett, a partner in Keener Oil Company, an independent oil company. Bartlett, shown here in 1967, served in the legislature, then became governor from 1967 to 1971. The next year, he was elected to the United States Senate. He died in 1979. (Courtesy Research Division of the Oklahoma Historical Society.)

John H. Williams, founder and chairman of the board of the Williams Companies, with pipeline and other energy operations nationwide, is the man most responsible for the revitalization of downtown Tulsa in the 1970s. In partnership with the city, he helped finance the redevelopment of a nine-block urban renewal area into the Williams Center, which includes the Performing Arts Center, office buildings, and the Williams headquarters. (Photography by Mary Beth, Inc., courtesy Williams.)

The tallest building in downtown Tulsa (shown at center) is a 52-story tower at One Williams Center. It serves as headquarters for Williams and the Bank of Oklahoma. The tower is an impressive sight for anyone looking north on Boston Avenue. The Williams Center, created by John H. Williams and the city of Tulsa, is one of the reasons Tulsa is considered one of the nation's most beautiful cities. (Courtesy Williams.)

One of the most successful accomplishments in the history of the Oklahoma petroleum industry has been a massive environmental effort to clean up well sites that had been abandoned many years ago. In 1993, oil leaders teamed with state officials to create the Oklahoma Energy Resources Board, a privatized state agency funded by a voluntary one-tenth of one percent assessment on oil and natural gas production. An example of a cleanup was this Hye project in Tulsa County. The before picture, shown above, shows concrete, trash, and debris, and the lower photograph shows the same area after it was returned to productive use. The work of the OERB has been a model for other oil producing states. (Courtesy Oklahoma Energy Resources Board.)

The cleanup of this area, called the Jackson Project in Okmulgee County, required the removal of concrete, tanks, trash, and debris. The before photograph (above) shows an old abandoned tank on a portion of the site, and the after photograph (below) indicates how the site looked after the cleanup. Between 1993 and 2004, the Oklahoma Energy Resources Board restored about 5,500 abandoned oil well sites in the state. Oklahoma has been a national leader in the petroleum industry's effort to improve the environment by cleaning up blighted sites, at a cost of about $3 million each year. Another major project of OERB is an educational program that provides petroleum industry materials and speakers to schools throughout the state. (Courtesy Oklahoma Energy Resources Board.)

In Glenpool, a growing suburb of Tulsa, a sign in front of the municipal building greets visitors with a Chamber of Commerce boast: "Welcome to Glenpool: The Town That Made Tulsa Famous." It was the discovery of the Glenn Pool, Oklahoma's first major oil field, that provided the impetus for the growth of Tulsa from a village into the city known for seven decades as the Oil Capital of the World.

The metal highway marker that stood at the intersection of U.S. Highway 75 and 141st Street in Glenpool, south of Tulsa, was replaced in 1995 by the Oklahoma Historical Society with this granite marker that commemorates the drilling of the Glenn Pool discovery well in 1905. In 2004, Glenpool was making plans for the centennial celebration of that event on November 22, 2005. Such an anniversary is certainly a cause for celebration not only in Glenpool but also in Tulsa and throughout the state.